The Dark Gnu

Wendy Videlock's poems contain laughing pears, rhyming coyotes, and jaded wind. In reading this book, I found myself laughing and gasping in equal measures. And cursing, as well, because Videlock is so damn good and I'm so damn jealous of her talent. She is one of my very favorite poets.

—Sherman Alexie

Reminiscent in some ways of Shel Silverstein's classic collections, Videlock's new book, The Dark Gnu and Other Poems, supplements sly whimsy with mystery and a hint of tragedy. These poems remind readers "of all inconceivable ages" that not all problems have solutions and that some narratives end in mystery rather than in resolution.

The Dark Gnu is enhanced by the author's illustrations that deepen the allure of the poems.

The voice is unmistakably Videlock's, but in this new collection we hear the echoes of Lewis Carroll and Edward Gorey.

These are the sorts of poems that children will demand to hear again and again and that parents will want to recite to each other and to their friends.

—Jeremy Telman

THE DARK GNU

AND OTHER POEMS

To Leslie, let there be estranging so wundm!

WRITTEN AND ILLUSTRATED BY
Wendy Videlock

ABLE MUSE PRESS

Copyright ©2013 by Wendy Videlock
First published in 2013 by

Able Muse Press

www.ablemusepress.com

Printed in the United States of America

Library of Congress Control Number: 2012951822

ISBN 978-1-927409-09-1 (paperback)
ISBN 978-1-927409-13-8 (hardcover)
ISBN 978-1-927409-10-7 (digital)

Cover & book design by Alexander Pepple

Cover image: *The Midnight Hour* by Wendy Videlock

Book illustrations by Wendy Videlock

Able Muse Press is an imprint of *Able Muse:* A Review of Poetry, Prose & Art—at
www.ablemuse.com

Able Muse Press
467 Saratoga Avenue #602
San Jose, CA 95129

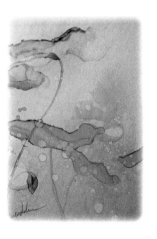

Acknowledgments

The author would like to acknowledge the support and generosity of Alex Pepple, the influence of Mother Goose, Strega Nona, and Mnemosyne, as well as the following publications, in which the following poems first appeared:

Able Muse: "The Road Cannot Make Up Her Mind."

Angle: "Pears."

Eleventh Muse: "About Certainty."

Kin Journal: "The Places You Have Been" (formerly "On Being Asked Where I Have Been").

Poetry: "If You're Crowish," "I Don't Buy It," "The Hawk," "Flowers."

Poetry Review: "Little by Little."

Quadrant "Some People."

The New Criterion: "To the Woman in the Garden."

"A Mammal Who" and "Oops" are found poems, with credit due *Animal Planet Magazine.*

"The Juggler of Gandaleen" was loosely adapted from old Irish, English, and Hebrew folktales.

CONTENTS

for shawn, sam, and the old man

I will show you fear in a handful of dust.

– T.S. Eliot

The Dark Gnu

An odd little book

for the drifters and dreamers,

the tygers and sages,

and the children of all

inconceivable ages.

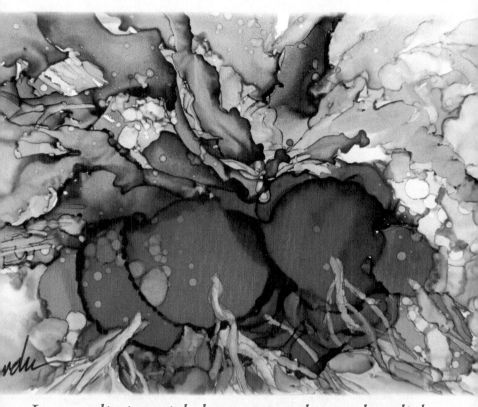

Let us distinguish between rules and radishes.

The First Poet:

Ugg.

You Might Have Noticed

You might have noticed the caterpillar
on your shoulder,
the badger who guards the gate,
the part of you that wants to run
and the part of you that waits,
the ghost that shadows you around
and changes who you are
from bird to foal to wooden bridge
to shooting little star.

The Road Cannot Make Up Her Mind

The road cannot make up her mind.
She wonders what you hope to find.
She's veering left, she's curving right,
she's climbing toward the open sky,
she's tunneling under the earth for a time.

Ayanna is always the name of the road.

She will give you the stone, and the buffalo.
She's pitching tents, demanding tolls
in valleys of singing and countries of bone,
with your hat full of joy and your boots full of snow,
for this is the way all roads will go.

A Kind of 'Ku

A dozen noisy blackbirds
are squabbling this afternoon.
The river keeps its cool.

The Quiet One

Where the needle of the compass
has quivered in the sun,
where the phantom finds the river
and asks where he is from,
where the leaf has fallen golden
and you think the day is done,
there stands the quiet one.

Oops

The dolphin's been
inspiring
oops
tattoos
for college girls
since '92.

What the Wind Said

You think you have it bad—

I have been pulling a thorn from my side
and the leaves from my ears
for a hundred million years.

Rupert

The day that Rupert crossed his eyes
and cracked an egg
against his head the people said

that man is mad,
he's corked his mind,
he's sunk his boat,
he's one slice shorter
than a loaf,
his fridge is hot,
he's lost the plot,
he's bonkers, wonky,
out of stew. . . .

Well, Rupert didn't say a word,
but took his daughter by the hand,
for Rupert knew a thing or two—
and Rupert knew his little girl

(who had been sad
for one whole day
and a half), could likely use
                              a little laugh.

You don't use your imagination; it uses you.

About Certainty

So much can be learned
from the open curve
of the question mark,
from the comma's calm,

from the certain *G*,
and the soft *w*,
from the kindred link
of the *q* and the *u*,

and yet,

and yet,

in this state,
a breath away
from the fervent curve,
from the *i* and the *u*

is the certain fear
of a kind of dark:
the abrupt chagrin,
the erasure mark.

The Island of Asleep

The winter wolf who journeyed to
The Island of Asleep
Returned a bearded peddler.

There were bells on his shoes,
Pearls in his teeth,
And scarves around his middle,

And bringing up the rear,
A wizard, a lynx, and a fiddler
Who swore they'd never heard

The huckleberry bird,
Nor been to the place in the sea
Known as the Island of Asleep.

I Don't Buy It

I don't buy it

says

the scientist.

Replies the frail

and faithful heart,

it's not for sale.

The Gypsy

The river people say
that in the blinding rain,
the gypsy takes the train,

which becomes a great giraffe
with starlings on its back
which turns into a vole
attended by a bat
with a legend for a map,
which blooms into a lake
which turns into a sleigh
which then becomes a swan

which turns into a plane
of garland and of glass
which rattles through the rain
and becomes a train again.

If You're Dappled

If you're dappled and you're clumsy,
if you're baffled half the time,
if you tend toward a circle
and it's hard to walk the line,

if you pause where there is music,
if you pocket little stones,
if you're with a thousand people
and you feel that you're alone,

if you have glimpsed a thread,
and a ghost has brought you the moon,
then you are of the floating kind
and we have been waiting for you.

A Mammal Who

The camel is a mammal who
would seem to understand
she is shaped by heat and sand.

The Guardians

An old medicine woman gave it to a man
with a bee upon his hand
who gave it to a brown child,
who gave it to a stalk of wheat
who passed it to a cobbler,
who gave it to a storyteller
who gave it to a poplar tree
who passed it then to me,
who passed it on to you,
who passed it on to one who
took it by the throat,

and rendered it a dove, drowned.
Do not fear.

A shepherd has taken the feathers to town.

Wherever you go, there is the moon.

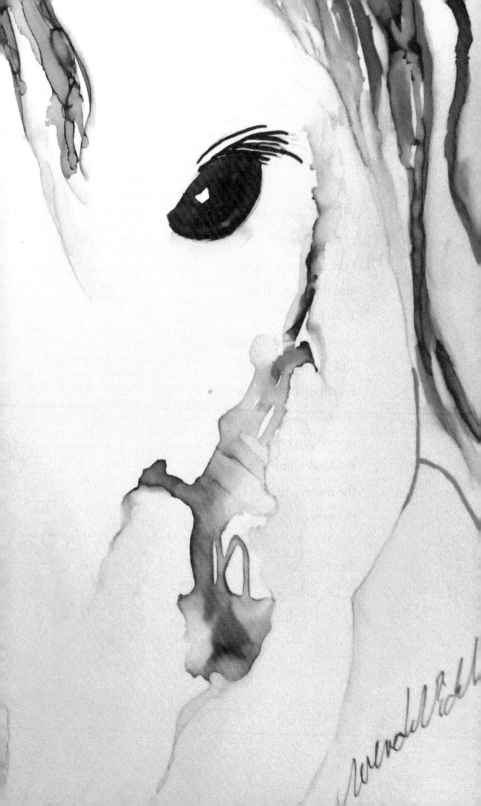

Let the Walrus In

Let the mountain in.
Let the spider in.
Let the sting and the wind
   and the seaweed in.
   Even let
   the dream and the ship
   and the sinking in.
   Feathers, antlers, claws,
   wings,
   moonlight creepers,
   shadows, djinns,
   the miners, the flyers, the waters,
   the hymns.

   Let them in
      Let them in
         Let them in.

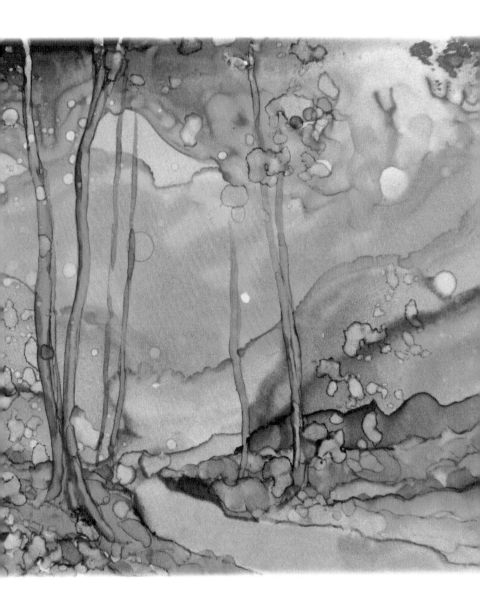

Flowers

They are fleeting.
They are fragile.
They require

little water.
They'll surprise you.
They'll remind you

that they aren't
and they are you.

31

The Lost One

What happened to your giggle, said
the goat to the mole,
did you take it out by the mulberry shed
and stuff it in a hole—
did you shove it under your rumpled bed
or hide it in a drawer,
did you swat it with The Sentinel
as it scuttled across the floor—
what's become of the other gold
when the laugh was in charge of the store. . . .

No matter, said the mole, so long
as it don't come back no more.

Some Places You Have Been

In a field of wheat,
on a dragon's tongue,
at the axiom

of a metaphor
and a bad pun,
at the loosening

of a baby tooth,

under a spell,
over the moon,
out of the blue,

at the quivering tip
of an arrow and
a bottom lip,

left behind,

at the canyon's rim,
on the spine of the wind,

let loose,

taken in.

Little By Little

Little by little the sparrow flies
toward the groaning epicenter
of a grand and historic twister,
and tumbling out on the other side,

silent as the lion's pride,
discovers the witch has already been squished,
the tornado story before has been told,
and the three wishes already wished

by the changeling and the angel of reeds,
who'd broken their bones and left their souls
in the mulberry limb, and the watering hole.

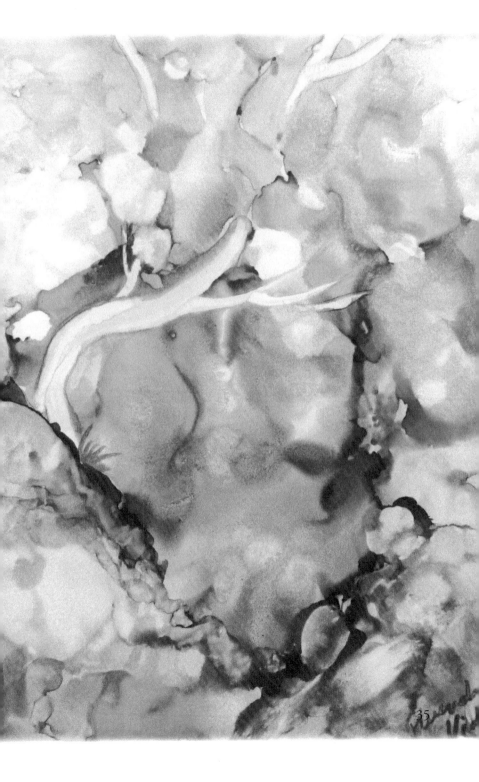

The Squirm

Watching a robin devour a worm
is enough to make you squirm,

as is saying you're sorry,
or tucking your tail,
or munching crow,
or eating your hat,

but

there are worse things,
there are far worse things than that.

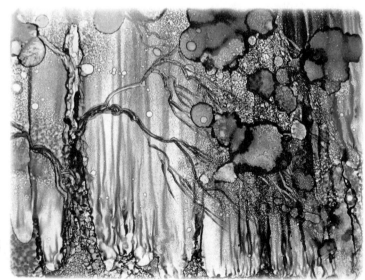

Fare Thee Well

Stay clear of Lake Superior,
go light in the Sea of Fears,
be still as a hint

at Rushing Creek
and long in the Zaire,
behold the gold at Crater Lake,
be hushed at Puget Sound,
go crooked through
the Bering Strait

where all the sails fall down—
and should the falcon come to you
with ribbons in her beak,

then don't forget
to count your sheep
and all the sounds
and all the seas

that you have known
before you fall asleep.

Everybody's got their own egg to hatch.

Said the Witch of Slain Valley

They wanted to see what I had on my walls.

They wanted to see the watering cans
hung from the ceilings,
the ones that overturn on the hour
and make the sounds of rain.

They wanted to borrow my cane and my hoof
and hobble the albino fields
where cauliflower and asparagus bloom,
there, in the upstairs room.
They wanted to hear the cathedral glass
bending beneath their feet
and lose their perfect ankles in
the clusters of golden maranta leaves
that spring from my kitchen floor.
They wanted to feel the quickening
and the crawling of the blackberry moss
that they might leave remembering
the stoop was sloped with maple leaves
and the doorbell was a moth.

Things that swim in deep waters

move slow,
don't you know
you might think

you might know
the spaces between think
and know, sleep
and go,
nowhere-ness,

and overflow,
overturned
and row, row, row,
glacier stone

and flake of snow,
hatchet fish
and spotted doe,
really fast
and oh,

so slow.

To the Woman in the Garden

You did not notice the roses,
the stones, or even
the toad, the child,
the sapling, the totem
pole, the crow, the dusk,
or the hummingbird,
the mantis, the dove,
or the hushed
word

but spoke instead,
but spoke at length
of the horrible
horrible
horrible world.

The Cunning One

By skillful means, tricks
and skulduggery,
rhyme,
roam
and rigamarole,

Coyote slips
through the keyhole.

Once upon a blue plume,

a great claw emerged,
a feather and a hoof,

a femur and a tooth,
a tendril and a word,

clear as a crystal pool
and dark as a darkling blur.

If Not for the Dark

If not for the dark,

no

spark.

Let there be shenanigans.

Star light, little star,

how strange
and far away you are.

The Dark Gnu

The dark gnus
clean their own
dirty hooves,
tend less

to blow the fuse,
move like
browns and blues,
find and lose,

graze, drift,
and peruse.

As You Would a Peach

In this poem
things are held loosely
as you would a peach.
There is no crate.
There are no feet.

Drink is another word
for sleep.
Bring your own lips.

Joey Sloan, roaming home, dreamed
he was a strawberry tree.
Ah, the sweet breeze.

His leaves were rain
and his limbs were long,
as long as the world could keep.

He woke with a start
at Willow Creek,
adjusted his tie,
and gratefully sighed,

Our fears are blue ships.
They worship their own sails.
It was then that he died,
but not before he turned to you.

Shhh . . .
I am the future's tool.
Be quiet, you are too.

Before the release, a cricket slips
out of the loop, onto your arm
and scurries in to know your palm.

You are a chime,
and the tiny stars scatter inside.

Your sadness is the arc of the sea,
the slope of the earth,
an old woman,
taking off her glasses.

The clock has taken all the straight lines,
and underneath, the moon slips.

Ah, the sweet breeze.

The Hawk

The forest is the only place
where green is green, and blue is blue.
Walking the forest I have seen
most everything. I've seen a you
with yellow eyes and busted wing.
And deep in the forest, no one knew.

A Flock of Words

A flock of words,
a big ol' moon—

put on your shoes
and gratitudes,
you gypsy moths,
you squirrelly fools,
stamp your hooves,
break
through,
you brightly colored
action verbs,
you squawking loons,
you hidden boons,
you tender little
earth
worms.

At Twenty After Caw

At twenty after caw
and half past moon
just before the center bead

was taken by the spool,
the great mother paused
her great mother loom
and halted the cosmic
elevator
at the elbow room.

Swivelled on a stool
in the elbow room
where Wednesday is a hare,
and color is a swerve,
where speed is a malady

and ceiling fans a cure,
where olives and almonds ever fall
in love like teenage girls,
where vigilance

and bitterness
depart their feather beds,
is where temperance
and dahlias
have come to rest their heads.

This is what the pause,
and the caw
and the spool
and the great mother said.

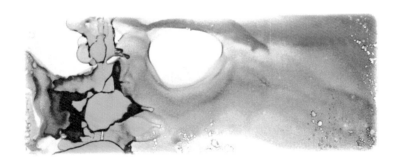

The Child with the Golden Thumb

Not really very far from here
nor even very long ago,
a child with a golden thumb,
a silver tooth, and a little mole

on the tip of his tongue
was shaken awake in the dead of night.
He did not know just why he woke,
what shook him never met his sight—

but all these things he did not know
collected in the morning light
and glistened in his little room
like freshly fallen flakes of snow.

A Bin of Pears

There's something sweetly weird
about a pear.
 It sits there, leaning
and uneven,
pearish
and speckled everywhere.

I swear
every pear
is laughing while it's sitting there.

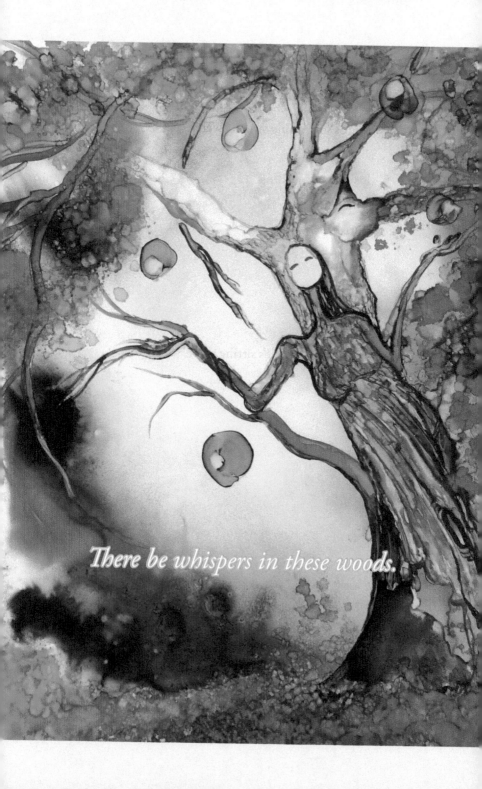

There be whispers in these woods.

Torganigan

Torganigan,
the great horned blue ape,
has crashed through the gates
and come through the floor,
has raided the feeder,
plundered the cellar,
and eaten the little dog next door.

It's said he did it all
with one fell swoop of the paw
and that he ate them all, raw.

Some people say Torganigan
is not an ape at all
but a rabid swan,
or a haggard wolf—
some say he is the ancient Beast
of Kelldagore,
who will not come again to feed
for a hundred years or more.

The Gnome Sage

The girl who didn't know her age
went to the home of the Gnome Sage.

Immediately she began losing things.
From her pockets fell a silver chain,
a thing that beeps, a couple of keys.

She even forgot her name.

Said the Gnome Sage,
Me too.
So very glad you came.

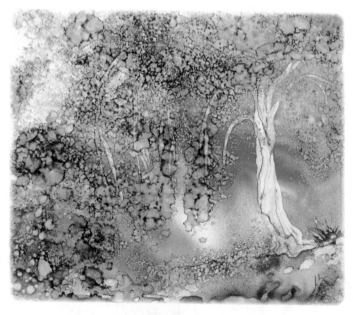

Cicada Methuselah Clan

Underground
they carry on,
but there is sound,

there's even song
that carries on
underground.

It is the sound
of underground,
of round and round,

of all fall down,
of sweet perceptions
and the sound

of small mouths sipping
underground.

Some People

Some people own a thousand books
and not one spine's been broken.
Some people speak and speak and speak

and not one word is spoken.
Some people fall for anything,
others fall to their knees.

Some people find me difficult.
Others call me a breeze.
Some people believe in miracles,

others are blank in the eye.
Some people pluck, some people seize,
and some are just waiting to die.

If You're Crowish

If you're crowish and you know it
give a caw

Caaaw

If you're weighted and you bear it,
send a moo

Moooo

If you're owl and you dreamed it,
give a hoo

Hoooo

If you're thirsty and you mean it
breathe an ahhh

Ahhh

You are putty in my hands

said the wind to the stone,

said the sun to the bloom,

said the darkness to the moon.

The Juggler from Gandaleen

More years ago than you can know
and twice as many as that
there lived a juggler from Gandaleen
who was neither wealthy nor fat.

So snug the juggler's hut, so small
his patch of floor, he could turn
the latch on the front door, clean
the kettle and the tin,

and lay his head to receive his dreams
without taking a step therein.
Beside his crumbling hut, a tree
with cherries the color of blood,

and blackbirds on the wing.
To the town's grassy roundabout
to the markets, weddings, and fairs
went the juggler with his pack on his back

and his swaying dappled mare,
where he juggled and danced for the children there
and he gave them his handmade wares
and he taught them to jig and he taught them to give

much to the people's despair—
for they scolded and scowled and sneered
at that juggler from Gandaleen
who did not save for his adage

nor charge for his trinkets and things
but juggled and danced for the little ones
and gave what he could give,
and the day would certainly come

when there'd be nothing left for him.
The spring turned into winter
and the summer had gone to the wind
and sure enough the time had arrived

for the juggler from Gandaleen,
who'd shared his bread with the mice and the birds
and given the children his things.
The people were sober and grim,

for they'd been right, they'd been right all along—
that simple juggler from Gandaleen—
there was nothing left for him.

Mortal-empty the juggler's belly,
and weak was he in the knee,
and out the door of his crumbling hut,
bare was the cherry tree.

But the juggler had a little song
that was tucked up into his sleeve
(for he'd had himself a mother
who'd been a bit of a dabbler

and she'd taught him a thing or three
about the river, and of dream).
The juggler sang that olden song
when he lay beneath the tree,

and as he closed his weary eyes
he summoned the spirits to take him,
or gift him the golden dream.

No sooner the witching hour had passed
and down from the cherry tree
slipped the Saint of Mercury
with a loaf of bread and some tea.

You must travel to Dulcimer town,
he said, *and sit yourself like a seer*
at the great stone by the river.
You shall hear what you need to hear.

The morning was cold and the juggler bemoaned
the journey that lay ahead,
but there was the kindly dappled mare,
and here was the tea and the bread.

Five days the juggler traveled
on the back of the swaying mare,
and the road was stirred with mice and birds
when the widow from Paris with stars in her hair

brought to the hungry juggler
a bowl of soup and some camembert.

When he entered the heart of Dulcimer town
he followed the road of the daughters,
(who will always lead to the waters),
and he sat himself down like a seer
at the great stone by the river.

And there he sat for hours and hours
in hopes the river would speak.
But nothing said the river,
and gone were the water bearers

and the only soul the juggler could see
was a seedy-looking merchant
who approached the hungry juggler
and sat down next to him.

Why's a scrawny pauper like you, he asked
sitting here like a seer
at the great stone by the river?

The juggler stepped to the water's edge
where the mare was drinking deep,
then he said to the merchant from Dulcimer,
I had myself a dream.

The merchant laughed and slapped his knee
in overdone hilarity,
a man he sneered, *who follows his dream*
is a foolish man indeed—
why just the other night I too
had myself a dream—

I dreamed the saint of Mercury
slipped through my door and said to me:

"There is a town called Gandaleen
and in that town there grows a tree
with cherries the color of blood
and blackbirds on the wing,
and buried underneath this tree
is a treasure filled with gold"—

Now what sort of fool would I be
if I heeded the saint of Mercury
and followed my dream to Gandaleen?
Beware, you scrawny pauper,
of the folly that dwells in dreams.

***

Well, perhaps I needn't tell you the rest
for chances are you've already guessed
how that scrawny juggler from Gandaleen
returned to his crumbling hut,
how he dropped to his knees at the base of the tree
with cherries the color of blood
and blackbirds on the wing,

how he lived to be grey and old,
how he juggled and danced and jigged—
and all the good that he did with the gold.

Sometimes

Sometimes I laugh at the wrong times.
I weep at the drop of a hat.
I've got a diamond up my sleeve,
and I'm striped as an alley cat.

My heart is a thing that comes unhinged,
and I can be blind as a bat.
I'm big as a moon inside my head
and almost as small as a gnat.

I'm told that I am not alone,
and others feel like that.

The Keepers

The grizzly keepers of the keys
have risen like ravens from the sea,
have given the aspen leaf the tree,

have given the circling hawk her scree,
have stirred your evening cup of tea,
have bent toward your every plea—

they have it in for you, and me—
the grizzly keepers of the keys.

An Invitation

I would like to invite you

to the place where reason meets

the beggar and the fool,

to the road where the mighty fleet

is a pebble in your shoe,

to the land where the darkness sweeps

the dust of what you knew,

to the stone where the mountain peaks

and falls away from view,

where the sword and the candle weep

for all that burns in you.

WENDY VIDELOCK lives on the Western Slope of the Colorado Rockies. Her full-length book of poems, *Nevertheless,* was released in 2011, and her chapbook, *What's That Supposed to Mean,* appeared in 2009. Her poems have been published widely in literary journals, most notably in *Poetry* and *The New York Times.*

ALSO FROM ABLE MUSE PRESS

Wendy Videlock, *Nevertheless - Poems*

Ben Berman, *Strange Borderlands - Poems*

Michael Cantor, *Life in the Second Circle - Poems*

Catherine Chandler, *Lines of Flight - Poems*

Margaret Ann Griffiths, *Grasshopper - The Poetry of M A Griffiths*

April Lindner, *This Bed Our Bodies Shaped - Poems*

James Pollock, *Sailing to Babylon - Poems*

Aaron Poochigian, *The Cosmic Purr - Poems*

Hollis Seamon, *Corporeality - Stories*

Matthew Buckley Smith, *Dirge for an Imaginary World - Poems*

Richard Wakefield, *A Vertical Mile - Poems*

Alexander Pepple, Editor, *Able Muse Anthology*

Alexander Pepple, Editor, *Able Muse - a review of poetry, prose & art,*
    issued semiannually since Winter, 2010

www.ablemusepress.com

CPSIA information can be obtained at www.ICGtesting.com
Printed in the USA
LVOW01s0335060913

351264LV00003B/5/P